WISE QUOTES: NAPOLEON BONAPARTE

(150 NAPOLEON BONAPARTE QUOTES)

Rowan Stevens

A commander-in-chief cannot take as an excuse for his mistakes in warfare an order given by his sovereign or his minister, when the person giving the order is absent from the field of operations and is imperfectly aware or wholly unaware of the latest state of affairs. It follows that any commander-in-chief who undertakes to carry out a plan which he considers defective is at fault; he must put forward his reasons, insist on the plan being changed, and finally tender his resignation rather than be the instrument of his army's downfall.

A commander-in-chief ought to say to himself several times a day: If the enemy should appear on my front, on my right, on my left, what would I do? And if the question finds him uncertain, he is not well placed, he is not as he should be, and he should remedy it.

A cowardly act! What do I care about that? You may be sure that I should never fear to commit one if it were to my advantage.

A form of government that is not the result of a long sequence of shared experiences, efforts, and endeavors can never take root.

A general must be a charlatan.

A good sketch is better than a long speech.

A great reserve and severity of manners are necessary for the command of those who are older than ourselves.

!

A leader is a dealer in hope.

A man does not have himself killed for a half pence a day or for a petty distinction. You must speak to the soul in order to electrify him.
A picture is worth a thousand words.

A revolution is an idea, taken up by bayonets.

A soldier will fight long and hard for a bit of colored ribbon.

!

A throne is only a bench covered with velvet.

A true man hates no one.

A woman laughing is a woman conquered.

Ability is of little account without opportunity.

Alexander, Caesar, Charlemagne, and I have founded empires. But on what did we rest the creations of our genius? Upon force. Jesus Christ founded his empire upon love; and at this hour millions of men would die for him.

*All celebrated people lose dignity upon a closer view.
All great events hang by a hair. The man of ability takes advantage of everything and neglects nothing that can give him a chance of success; whilst the less able man sometimes loses everything by neglecting a single one of those chances.*

Always carry champagne! In victory you deserve it and in defeat you need it!

Among so many conflicting ideas and so many different perspectives, the honest man is confused and distressed and the skeptic becomes wicked ... Since one must take sides, one might as well choose the side that is victorious, the side which devastates, loots, and burns. Considering the alternative, it is better to eat than to be eaten.

An army marches on its stomach.

As a rule, it is circumstances that make men.

As for me, to love you alone, to make you happy, to do nothing which would contradict your wishes, this is my destiny and the meaning of my life.

At the beginning of a campaign it is important to consider whether or not to move forward; but when one has taken the offensive it is necessary to maintain it to the last extremity. However skillfully effected a retreat may be, it always lessens the morale of an army, since in losing the chances of success, they are remitted to the enemy. A retreat, moreover, costs much more in men and materials than the bloodiest engagements, with this difference, also, that in a battle the enemy loses practically as much as you do; while in a retreat you lose and he does not.

Audacity succeeds as often as it fails; in life it has an even chance.

China is a sleeping giant. Let her sleep, for when she wakes she will move the world.

Circumstances-what are circumstances? I make circumstances.

Conquests will come and go but Delambre's work will endure.

Courage cannot be counterfeited. It is one virtue that escapes hypocrisy.

Courage is like love, it must have hope for nourishment.

Courage isn't having the strength to go on - it is going on when you don't have strength.

Death is nothing, but to live defeated and inglorious is to die daily.

England is a nation of shopkeepers.

Force cannot organize anything. In the long run, the sword is always beaten by the spirit by which I mean the civil and religious institutions of a nation.
Four hostile newspapers are more to be feared than a thousand bayonets.

From triumph to downfall there is but one step. I have noted that, in the most momentous occasions, mere nothings have always decided the outcome of the greatest events.

Give me enough medals and I'll win you any war.

Glory is fleeting, but obscurity is forever.

Great ambition is the passion of a great character. Those endowed with it may perform very good or bad acts. All depends on the principles which direct them.

Great men are meteors designed to burn so that earth may be lighted.

Greatness is nothing unless it be lasting.

He who cannot look over a battlefield with a dry eye, causes the death of many men uselessly.

He who fears being conquered is sure of defeat.

History is a set of lies agreed upon.

History is written by the winners.

!

I am surrounded by priests who repeat incessantly that their kingdom is not of this world, and yet they lay hands on everything they can get.

I have seen only you, I have admired only you, I desire only you.

I hope before long to press you in my arms and shall shower on you a million burning kisses as under the Equator.

I know he's a good general, but is he lucky?

!

I make my battle plans from the spirit of my sleeping soldiers.

I saw the crown of France laying on the ground, so I picked it up with my sword.

I start out by believing the worst.

If I had to choose a religion, the sun as the universal giver of life would be my god.

If the art of war were nothing but the art of avoiding risks, glory would become the prey of mediocre minds.... I have made all the calculations; fate will do the rest.

If they want peace, nations should avoid the pin-pricks that precede cannon shots.

If we could read the past histories of all our enemies we would disregard all hostility for them.

If you want a thing done well, do it yourself.

If you wish to be a success in the world, promise everything, deliver nothing.

Imagination governs the world.

Impossible is the word found only in a fool's dictionary. Wise people create opportunities for themselves and make everything possible.

In Love, Victory goes to the man who runs away.

In our time no one has the conception of what is great. It is up to me to show them.

In politics nothing is immutable. Events carry within them an invincible power. The unwise destroy themselves in resistance. The skillful accept events, take strong hold of them and direct them.

In politics, stupidity is not a handicap.

In war, the moral is to the physical as ten to one.
In war, theory is all right so far as general principles are concerned; but in reducing general principles to practice

there will always be danger. Theory and practice are the axis about which the sphere of accomplishment revolves.

It is a mistake, too, to say that the face is the mirror of the soul. The truth is, men are very hard to know, and yet, not to be deceived, we must judge them by their present actions, but for the present only.

It is not that addresses at the opening of a battle make the soldiers brave. The old veterans scarcely hear them, and recruits forget them at the first boom of the cannon. Their usefulness lies in their effect on the course of the campaign, in neutralizing rumors and false reports, in maintaining a good spirit in the camp, and in furnishing matter for camp-fire talk. The printed order of the day should fulfill these different ends.

It is not true that men never change; they change for the worse, as well as for the better. It is not true they are ungrateful; more often the benefactor rates his favors higher than their worth; and often too he does not allow for circumstances. If few men have the moral force to resist impulses, most men do carry within themselves the germs of virtues as well as of vices, of heroism as well as of cowardice. Such is human nature — education and circumstances do the rest.

It is only by prudence, wisdom, and dexterity, that great ends are attained and obstacles overcome. Without these qualities nothing succeeds.

It is the cause, not the death, that makes the martyr.

It requires more courage to suffer than to die.

It's the unconquerable soul of man, and not the nature of the weapon he uses, that ensures victory.

Lead the ideas of your time and they will accompany and support you; fall behind them and they drag you along with them; oppose them and they will overwhelm you.

Let France have good mothers, and she will have good sons.

Let her sleep, for when she wakes, she will shake the world.

Men are more easily governed through their vices than through their virtues.

Men are Moved by two levers only: fear and self-interest.

Men have their virtues and their vices, their heroisms and their perversities; men are neither wholly good nor wholly bad, but possess and practice all that there is of good and bad here below. Such is the general rule. Temperament, education, the accidents of life, are modifying factors. Outside of this, everything is ordered arrangement, everything is chance. Such has been my rule of expectation and it has usually brought me success.

Men of great ambition have sought happiness . . . and have found fame.

Morality has nothing to do with such a man as I am.

More glorious to merit a sceptre than to possess one.

!

Music is what tell us that the human race is greater than we realize.

Never depend on the multitude, full of instability and whims; always take precautions against it.

Never interrupt your enemy when he is making a mistake.

Never tell your enemy he is doing the wrong thing.

Nothing is lost as long as courage remains.

Nothing is more difficult, and therefore more precious, than to be able to decide.

One is more certain to influence men, to produce more effect on them, by absurdities than by sensible ideas.

One must indeed be ignorant of the methods of genius to suppose that it allows itself to be cramped by forms. Forms are for mediocrity, and it is fortunate that mediocrity can act only according to routine. Ability takes its flight unhindered.

One must learn to forgive and not to hold a hostile, bitter attitude of mind, which offends those about us and prevents us from enjoying ourselves; one must recognize human shortcomings and adjust himself to them rather than to be constantly finding fault with them.

Orders and decorations are necessary in order to dazzle the people.

Ordinarily men exercise their memory much more than their judgment.

!

Power is my mistress. I have worked too hard at her conquest to allow anyone to take her away from me.

Put your iron hand in a velvet glove.

Religion is excellent stuff for keeping common people quiet.

Religion is what keeps the poor from murdering the rich.

Show me a family of readers, and I will show you the people who move the world.

Society is impossible without inequality, inequality intolerable without a code of morality, and a code of morality unacceptable without religion.
Success is the most convincing talker in the world.

Take time to deliberate, but when the time for action comes, stop thinking and go in.

Ten people who speak make more noise than ten thousand who are silent.

!

The battlefield is a scene of constant chaos. The winner will be the one who controls that chaos, both his own and the enemies.

The best cure for the body is a quiet mind.

The best way to keep one's word is not to give it.

The extent of your consciousness is limited only by your ability to love and to embrace with your love the space around you, and all it contains.

The fool has one great advantage over a man of sense — he is always satisfied with himself.

The great mass of society are far from being depraved; for if a large majority were criminal or inclined to break the laws, where would the force or power be to prevent or constrain them? And herein is the real blessing of civilization, because this happy result has its origin in her bosom, growing out of her very nature.

The greater the man, the less is he opinionative, he depends upon events and circumstances.

The greatest danger occurs at the moment of victory.

The hand that gives is among the hand that takes. Money has no fatherland, financiers are without patriotism and without decency, their sole object is gain.

The herd seek out the great, not for their sake but for their influence; and the great welcome them out of vanity or need.

The laws of circumstance are abolished by new circumstances.

The most difficult art is not in the choice of men, but in giving to the men chosen the highest service of which they are capable.

The nature of strategy consists of always having, even with a weaker army, more forces at the point of attack or at the point where one is being attacked than the enemy.

The only victories which leave no regret are those which are gained over ignorance.

The only victory over love is flight.

!

The reason most people fail instead of succeed is they trade what they want most for what they want at the moment.

The surest way to remain poor is to be honest.

The world suffers a lot. Not because the violence of bad people. But because of the silence of the good people.

There are in the world, two powers. The sword and the spirit. The spirit has always vanquished the sword.

!

There are so many laws that no one is safe from hanging.

There are two levers for moving man -- interest and fear.
There is a joy in danger.

There is no place in a fanatic's head where reason can enter.

There shall be no Alps.

This soldier, I realized, must have had friends at home and in his regiment; yet he lay there deserted by all except his dog. I looked on, unmoved, at battles which decided the future of nations. Tearless, I had given orders which brought death to thousands. Yet here I was stirred, profoundly stirred, stirred to tears. And by what? By the grief of one dog.

Those who receive the most images into their memories have the most lively imaginations.

Throw off your worries when you throw off your clothes at night.

To understand the man you have to know what was happening in the world when he was twenty.

To write history one must be more than a man, since the author who holds the pen of this great justiciary must be free from all preoccupation of interest or vanity.

True character stands the test of emergencies. Do not be mistaken, it is weakness from which the awakening is rude.

Variety made the Revolution. Liberty was just a pretext.

Victory belongs to the most persevering.

War is becoming an anachronism; if we have battled in every part of the continent it was because two opposing social orders were facing each other, the one which dates from 1789, and the old regime. They could not exist together; the younger devoured the other. I know very well, that, in the final reckoning, it was war that overthrew me, me the representative of the French Revolution, and the instrument of its principles. But no matter! The battle was lost for civilization, and civilization will inevitably take its revenge. There are two systems, the past and the future. The present is only a painful transition. Which must triumph? The future, will it not? Yes indeed, the future! That is, intelligence, industry, and peace. The past was brute force, privilege, and ignorance. Each of our victories was a triumph for the ideas of the Revolution. Victories will be won, one of these days, without cannon, and without bayonets.

War is the business of barbarians.

Water, air, and cleanness are the chief articles in my pharmacy.

We are made weak both by idleness and distrust of ourselves. Unfortunate, indeed, is he who suffers from both. If he is a mere individual he becomes nothing; if he is a king he is lost.

We frustrate many designs against us by pretending not to see them.

We must laugh at man to avoid crying for him.

What are the conditions that make for the superiority of an army? Its internal organization, military habits in officers and men, the confidence of each in themselves; that is to say, bravery, patience, and all that is contained in the idea of moral means.

What is a throne? — a bit of wood gilded and covered in velvet. I am the state— I alone am here the representative of the people. Even if I had done wrong you should not have reproached me in public—people wash their dirty linen at home. France has more need of me than I of France.

What is the government? Nothing, unless supported by opinion.

When a government is dependent upon bankers for money, they and not the leaders of the government control the situation, since the hand that gives is above the hand that takes. Money has no motherland; financiers are without patriotism and without decency; their sole object is gain.

When you have an enemy in your power, deprive him of the means of ever injuring you.

You can ask me for anything you like, except time.

You don't govern men who don't have religion, you shoot them.

You don't reason with intellectuals. You shoot them.

You tell me that class distinctions are baubles used by monarchs, I defy you to show me a republic, ancient or modern, in which distinctions have not existed. You call these medals and ribbons baubles; well, it is with such baubles that men are led. I would not say this in public, but in a assembly of wise statesmen it should be said. I don't think that the French love liberty and equality: the French are not changed by ten years of revolution: they are what the Gauls were, fierce and fickle. They have one feeling: honour. We must nourish that feeling. The people clamour for distinction. See how the crowd is awed by the medals and orders worn by foreign diplomats. We must recreate these distinctions. There has been too much tearing down; we must rebuild. A government exists, yes and power, but the nation itself - what is it? Scattered grains of sand.

You would make a ship sail against the winds and currents by lighting a bonfire under her decks? I have no time for such nonsense.

www.ingramcontent.com/pod-product-compliance
Lightning Source LLC
Chambersburg PA
CBHW071255070526
44583CB00017B/2487